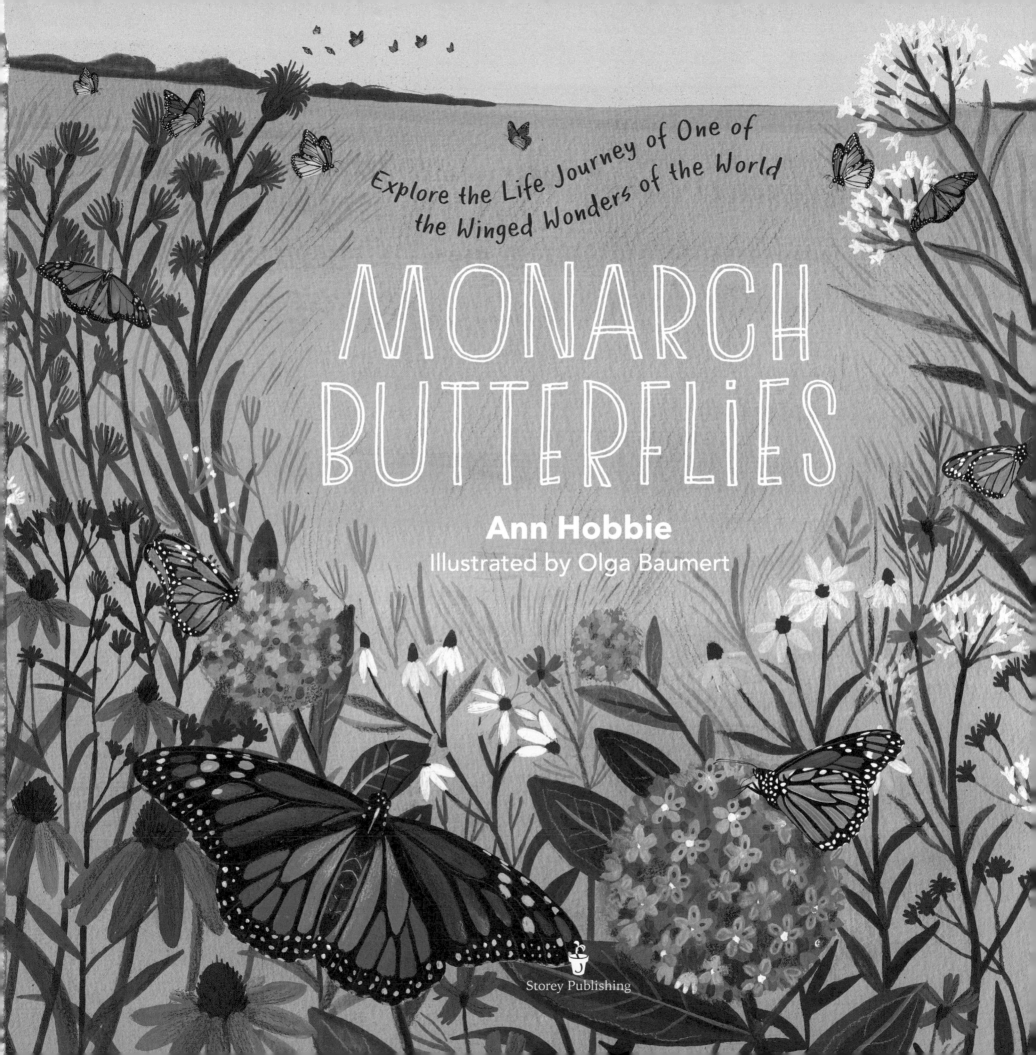

Explore the Life Journey of One of
the Winged Wonders of the World

MONARCH
BUTTERFLIES

Ann Hobbie

Illustrated by Olga Baumert

Storey Publishing

Contents

It All Begins with an Egg, 4

The Larval Life, 6

Anatomy of a Caterpillar, 8

A Magical Metamorphosis, 10

Anatomy of a Chrysalis, 11

A Grand Entrance, 12

Anatomy of a Butterfly, 14

Marvelous Milkweed, 16

Busy Life in the Milkweed Patch, 18

Summer on the Wing, 20

The Journey South, 22

Where Do They Go?, 24

Fuel for the Flight, 25

¡Hola, Mariposas!, 26

A Just-Right Place, 28

The Final Flight, 30

Monarchs in the West, 32

Monarchs in Danger, 34

Everything Is Connected, 36

Help the Monarchs on Their Journey, 38

How to Rear a Monarch, 40

Fun Facts, 43

Glossary, 44

Going Deeper, 45

Index, 47

It All Begins with an Egg

The amazing life of a monarch butterfly begins with a tiny white egg hidden on the underside of a leaf. A mother monarch lays her eggs only on milkweed plants. When her caterpillar babies hatch, milkweed is all they will eat.

The mother butterfly will probably lay just one egg on each milkweed plant, but in her lifetime she will lay as many as 300 to 500 eggs.

Eggs have pointed tips and ridged sides.

The monarch mother makes her egg sticky so that it stays on the leaf even in wind and rain.

When the caterpillar is ready to hatch, you can see its black head through the shell.

The Larval Life

After only a few days, the tiny white caterpillar, also called a *larva*, nibbles its way out of its shell and wriggles onto the leaf. The caterpillar's first meal is its own eggshell. Then it will munch on milkweed nonstop for nearly two weeks, growing bigger and bigger. It will grow so much that it will *molt*, or outgrow its own skin, five times!

The stages between molts are called *instars*. Can you spot each instar? How is the caterpillar changing?

After a day or two, the caterpillar has yellow, black, and white stripes.

Tiny *tentacles* get larger as the caterpillar grows.

When a monarch molts, it becomes wrinkly and still. It scoots out of its skin and pops off its head capsule like a face mask! The growing caterpillar eats the old skin left behind.

Silk trapeze! Sometimes, to help it hold on in rough weather or escape from danger, the caterpillar hangs from a strong silk string that it makes with its **spinneret**.

The caterpillar will grow to 2,000 times its original size! What is 2,000 times your birth weight?

ANATOMY OF A CATERPILLAR

Tentacles. These help the caterpillar find its way around.

Thorax. This section contains all the parts that will become the upper part of the butterfly's body, including the wings.

Abdomen. The caterpillar's abdomen will become the butterfly's abdomen.

The rear tentacles might confuse predators into thinking the caterpillar's back end is its head.

Head

True legs. These are the legs that the monarch will keep when it's a butterfly.

Spiracles. Caterpillars breathe through these tiny holes. Look closely and you can see them!

Prolegs. These legs will disappear in adulthood. They have little hooks on their tips that help the caterpillar crawl along.

When you pick up a caterpillar, it might "play possum," curling up in a tight ball.

CLOSE-UP OF THE HEAD

Head capsule. Every time it molts, the caterpillar sheds its head capsule.

After shedding its skin for the fifth and last time, the larva weighs more than the adult butterfly will!

Ocelli. Even with these 12 tiny eyes, the caterpillar has terrible eyesight!

Antennae. When the larva becomes a butterfly, it will grow long antennae from these tiny nubs.

Maxillary palps. These help the caterpillar sense and find food as it crawls about.

Spinneret. The caterpillar uses the spinneret to spin strings of silk. It makes a silk pad to hang from when it forms a chrysalis.

Mandibles. These mouthparts are for munching all that milkweed.

A Magical Metamorphosis

The full-grown monarch caterpillar is finally ready for a complete change, or a **metamorphosis**. Not many people get to see this happen in the wild, but it is amazing to watch!

First, the caterpillar climbs under a sturdy surface. Using its spinneret, it spins a silk pad and holds on with its last pair of legs. The caterpillar hangs upside-down in a J shape.

After a day, the J-shaped caterpillar goes limp. Its tentacles become loose ringlets. Beginning at its head, its wrinkled skin begins to split.

The monarch wriggles out from its rumpled skin one last time before becoming a glorious green **chrysalis**. The chrysalis is also called a pupa. This part of metamorphosis is called **pupation**.

ANATOMY OF A CHRYSALIS

The monarch will stay in the chrysalis for 9 to 14 days.
Amazing changes are happening inside!

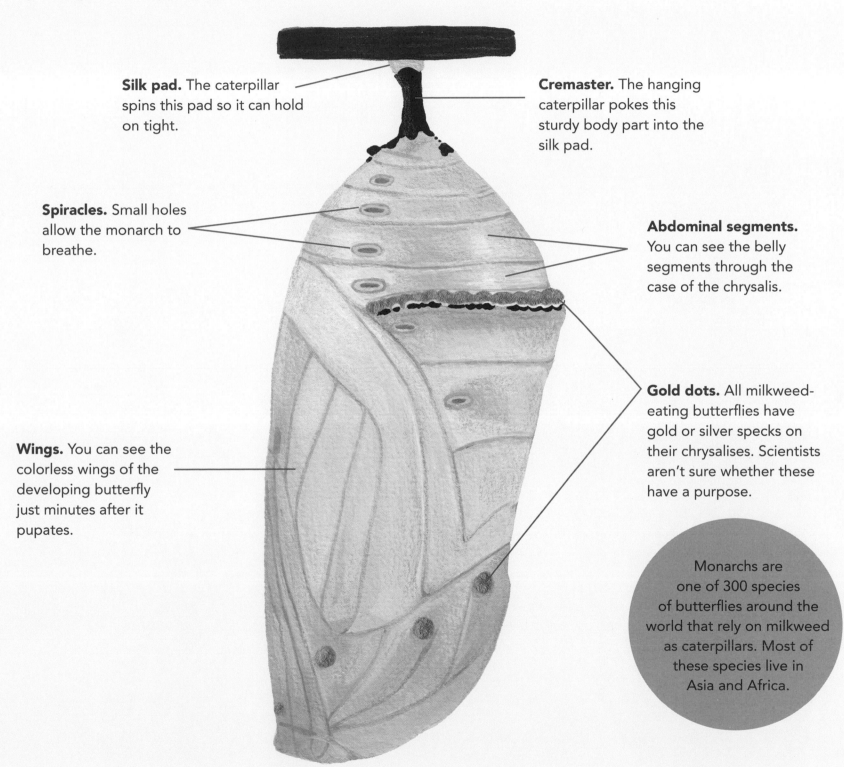

Silk pad. The caterpillar spins this pad so it can hold on tight.

Cremaster. The hanging caterpillar pokes this sturdy body part into the silk pad.

Spiracles. Small holes allow the monarch to breathe.

Abdominal segments. You can see the belly segments through the case of the chrysalis.

Gold dots. All milkweed-eating butterflies have gold or silver specks on their chrysalises. Scientists aren't sure whether these have a purpose.

Wings. You can see the colorless wings of the developing butterfly just minutes after it pupates.

Monarchs are one of 300 species of butterflies around the world that rely on milkweed as caterpillars. Most of these species live in Asia and Africa.

A Grand Entrance

When it's finally time for the monarch to become a butterfly, the chrysalis appears to darken. Inside, the tiny scales that cover the butterfly's body and wings turn black, orange, and white.

Just before it *ecloses*, or hatches, the monarch draws in air through its spiracles to pop open the case so it can crawl out.

You can see the butterfly's colorful wings folded up inside the clear casing.

The butterfly clings to the case, its wings still crinkled. It is pumping **hemolymph**, or insect blood, from its body out to the wings. The wings unfurl like beautiful velvet.

The brand-new monarch hangs for several hours before flying off to look for nectar.

ANATOMY OF A BUTTERFLY

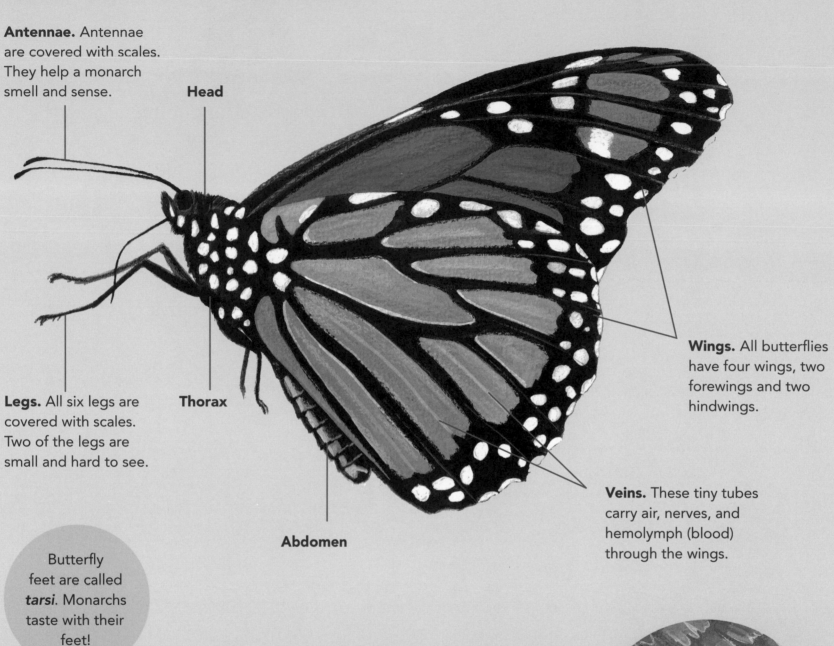

Antennae. Antennae are covered with scales. They help a monarch smell and sense.

Head

Legs. All six legs are covered with scales. Two of the legs are small and hard to see.

Thorax

Abdomen

Wings. All butterflies have four wings, two forewings and two hindwings.

Veins. These tiny tubes carry air, nerves, and hemolymph (blood) through the wings.

Butterfly feet are called *tarsi*. Monarchs taste with their feet!

Scales of different shapes, sizes, and colors cover the monarch's whole body. These scales make the beautiful patterns on the wings. They also help the butterfly fly and absorb the sun's warmth.

CLOSE-UP OF THE HEAD

Palpi. These ridges are covered with furlike scaly sensors that monarchs use to smell.

Antennae

Eyes. The eyes are made up of thousands of lenses. Monarchs have fantastic vision!

Proboscis. The monarch unrolls this tube to soak up flower nectar and water.

MALE OR FEMALE?

On the inside of a male monarch's hind wings are two black dots. Males also have organs called *claspers* on the tips of their abdomens.

male

Females are a bit duller orange than males, with thicker black wing veins. A female has a V-shaped indentation near the end of her abdomen.

female

Marvelous Milkweed

Milkweed is key to the life of a monarch. The butterfly can't survive without it. There are more than 100 kinds of milkweed in North America! At first glance, they might not look much alike. But if you look very closely, you will see the things they all have in common.

swamp milkweed

antelope horn milkweed

Tiny flowers grow in clusters. Each flower has five petals pointing up and five pointing down.

butterfly milkweed

narrow-leaf milkweed

The leaves are thick and have a vein down the middle. The bottoms are paler than the tops.

Inside the leaves is a milky, sticky sap that is toxic to many animals but not to monarchs.

Common milkweed grows in all sorts of places —
prairies, ditches, roadsides, and even cracks in
the sidewalk. What kinds of milkweed grow
where you live? Take a sniff of their flowers.
Some milkweeds smell wonderful!

common
milkweed

After the flowers die back,
long pods release fluffy seeds
that float on the wind.

Busy Life in the Milkweed Patch

Before becoming a butterfly, a monarch caterpillar's world is the bustling milkweed patch it shares with oodles of other creatures, many of which eat milkweed too.

bumblebee

great spangled fritillary

katydid

sharpshooter leafhopper

tachinid fly

Bees, beetles, moths, and other butterflies drink the sweet juices of milkweed flowers. Katydids, lacewings, and leafhoppers rest on milkweed plants. A gray tree frog lies in wait to snatch up a fly for its lunch.

eastern gray tree frog

The milkweed patch is also home to many critters that eat monarchs! Stink bugs, tachinid flies, fire ants, wasps, and jumping spiders all eat monarch eggs, caterpillars, or chrysalises.

stink bug

jumping spider

ladybug

fire ant

aphids

Summer on the Wing

When a monarch becomes a butterfly, the life cycle begins again. A new *brood* of monarchs develops each month, as long as there is milkweed, until the last days of summer. These summer butterflies live for about one month as adults. They flit around gardens and fields in the endless work of survival.

If you look carefully, you can be a monarch detective. What are they up to?

Monarchs mate! Male monarchs chase females. A pair will roost in a tree and stay together until sunrise the next day.

Female monarchs *oviposit*, or lay eggs. Watch for females landing on milkweed and tucking their abdomens under a leaf.

Monarchs drink nectar! They go from flower to flower, tasting with their feet and unrolling their proboscis to drink.

POLLINATOR POWER

While looking for nectar, monarchs help spread pollen grains from flower to flower. This is how plants make fruits and seeds. Moths, bees, flies, beetles, hummingbirds, and bats also help *pollinate* flowers.

The Journey South

In late summer, days get shorter. Nights get longer and cooler. The milkweed yellows and dries. These signals tell the monarchs that winter will come and it's time to leave. They must find a safe place to rest until milkweed comes up in the spring.

Monarchs born
at this time look the
same as the summer butterflies,
but their lives will be much different, and
much longer. They will live for up to nine
months! Instead of mating and laying eggs, these
special monarchs will *migrate* south for winter.

Over several months, monarchs soar over cities, farms, and lakes. They glide over hillsides, forests, and river valleys. Traveling some 20 miles each day, they drink from as many flowers as they can find. As they travel south, more and more butterflies join the journey.

As the sun goes down each day, the monarchs fly up into the trees to find each other and roost together for the night.

Where Do They Go?

The migrating monarchs have never made this trip before. How do they know where to go? Scientists have found that they use the sun and the mountains to figure out which direction to fly.

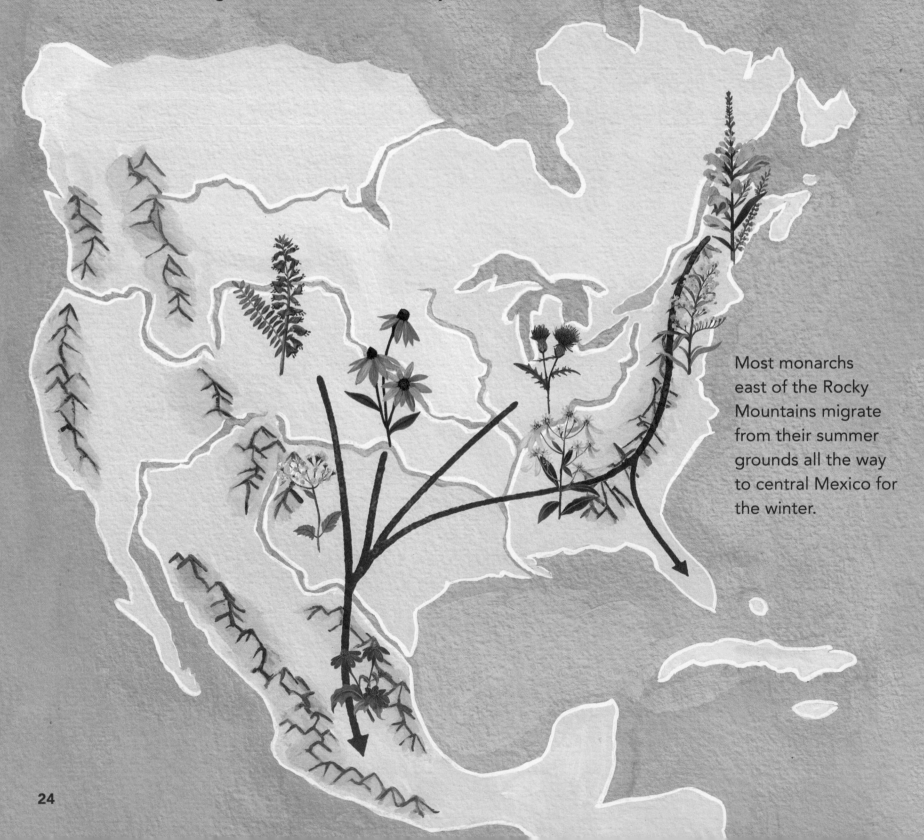

Most monarchs east of the Rocky Mountains migrate from their summer grounds all the way to central Mexico for the winter.

Fuel for the Flight

During their migration, monarchs drink the nectar of many fall-blooming flowers to give them energy for the long trip to Mexico.

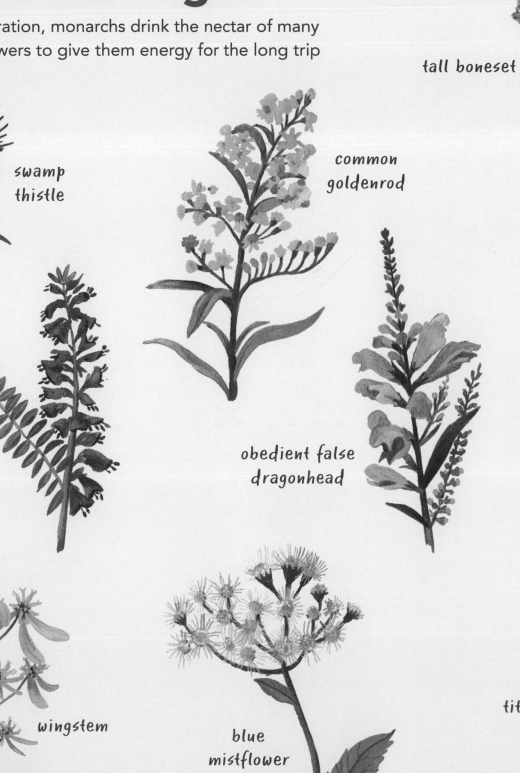

tall boneset

swamp thistle

common goldenrod

leadplant

black-eyed Susan

obedient false dragonhead

wingstem

blue mistflower

tithonia

¡Hola, Mariposas!

By early November, millions of monarch butterflies begin to arrive in the mountains of central Mexico. They will settle here for the winter. Some monarchs have flown nearly 3,000 miles to get here! In Spanish, the word for butterfly is *mariposa*.

On November 1 and 2, people in Mexico celebrate a holiday called Día de los Muertos, or Day of the Dead. They build altars called *ofrendas* at home and at grave sites to honor and welcome loved ones who have died. Many people believe monarchs are a symbol of the spirits of the dead coming back to visit.

There are parades and parties, costumes and ceremonies, music, and plenty of food, tears, and laughter!

A Just-Right Place

Finally, the weary monarchs can rest! They have reached the south-facing slopes of Mexico's transvolcanic mountain range. These monarchs are here for the first time, but their great-great-grandparents gathered here last winter. Monarchs have probably been making this journey for thousands of years.

Millions of monarchs roost in the oyamel fir trees. Branches bend under their weight. Even the trunks are covered with speckled butterflies.

But even in the quiet oyamel forests, life is hard. Some monarchs are eaten by mice or birds. Some get knocked down by storms. Others simply run out of energy and can't survive.

29

The Final Flight

It's spring in Mexico! As spring days get longer and warmer, the monarchs get ready to fly north again. One sunny day in March, a few butterflies take flight and begin to mate. Over the following weeks, thousands of butterflies stream down the mountainside and then lift high into the air.

The tired, hungry monarchs use the last of their strength to search for nectar and milkweed as they head north toward northern Mexico, Texas, Louisiana, and Arkansas.

Once they've laid their eggs, the long lives of these migrators come to an end. Their children will continue the journey north, beginning the cycle all over again.

The people of the nearby towns say goodbye to the monarchs. Next year they will welcome the butterflies' great-great-grandchildren!

Monarchs in the West

Not all monarchs migrate to Mexico. Most monarchs that live west of the Rocky Mountains fly to a different place when nights get cold: the coast of California. They spend the winter in groves of pine, cypress, eucalyptus, and other trees. When spring comes, they fly inland again to find milkweed.

These are a few of the western monarchs' favorite flowers.

mountain monardella

California goldenrod

Rocky Mountain bee plant

common sunflower

Most western monarchs migrate to California, but a few also go to Mexico. Likewise, most eastern monarchs fly to Mexico, but a few head to California.

There aren't very many western monarchs anymore. The dry plains, big mountains, and deserts of the West make it hard for milkweed to grow. Sometimes, the trees the monarchs overwinter in are cut down. Storms, droughts, floods, and wildfires are hard on them. And there aren't enough flowers to drink from. To help, many people are planting the flowers that monarchs need to survive.

People plant flowers along roadsides and in yards, school grounds, and parks.

Monarchs in Danger

Monarchs have a lot of *predators* — insects, spiders, birds, and mammals who eat them. Predators are natural in the cycle of wild things. But people also harm monarchs, even if they don't mean to.

Sometimes monarch *habitat* is destroyed to build houses and roads.

Many farmers use weed killers and other **pesticides** to grow crops, but these chemicals are poisonous to milkweed and butterflies.

Some farmers plant native plants, shrubs, and flowering trees around their fields and orchards to feed monarchs and other **pollinators** that help their crops grow.

People can hurt monarchs, but people can help monarchs, too. See page 38 to find out how you can help monarchs near you.

Everything Is Connected

Monarch butterflies are both tough and delicate, tiny and tremendous.
At each stage in their lives, monarchs share habitat with hundreds of
other plants and animals, who in turn share their worlds with hundreds
more. When a monarch's habitat is poisoned or destroyed, many other
important creatures struggle too.

When we make sure monarchs have the milkweed, nectar flowers, and roosting trees they need, we are also caring for all the other pollinators, predators, and animals who need the same flowers and trees — and each other — to survive.

The monarchs' wrinkled stripes and royal wings remind us that we are part of an amazing web of life.

Help the Monarchs on Their Journey

A monarch's journey can be hard and dangerous. The good news is that there are a lot of things you can do to help the monarchs near you!

Build Habitat

The best way to help is make more monarch habitat — great places for them to live. Ask a grown-up to take you to your local plant nursery, where you can buy plants that butterflies like. These should include native plants, the kind that grow best right where you live.

Plant milkweed, even in the city! Milkweed likes to grow anywhere: yards, alleys, roadside ditches, farm borders, schools, churches, park edges, and under power lines.

Plant flowering perennials, plants that come back every spring. Choose flowers that bloom at different times of year so that there's always nectar for insects to drink, whether it's spring, summer, or fall.

Plant annual flowers each spring. Annuals bloom all summer long, then die in the fall when the weather gets cold. (Ask the nursery or grower if the annuals are safe for insects.)

A PESKY PLANT

People often plant colorful tropical milkweed hoping to help monarchs. But it's not native in most places where people plant it, and it often doesn't die back in winter. It attracts so many monarchs that it gets covered with a nasty monarch disease called OE (*Ophryocystis elektroscirrha* . . . it's a mouthful!). The caterpillars can catch it when they eat the contaminated milkweed. Please don't plant tropical milkweed!

Be a Community Scientist

You can help scientists learn more about monarchs by being a good observer of the monarchs right where you live. See page 45 to learn more about the organizations mentioned below.

Catch and tag monarchs to see where they go! Scientists rely on volunteers around the country to tag monarchs with stickers every fall. People find monarchs with these tiny stickers along their migration routes. The stickers tell the scientists where the monarchs started their journey. Order tags from Southwest Monarch Study (southwestern states) or Monarch Watch (eastern states). Unfortunately, it is illegal to handle monarchs in California because their numbers are so low.

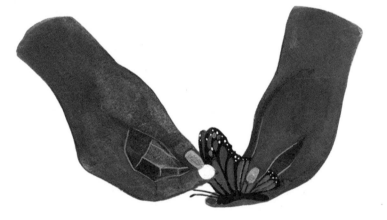

Adopt a milkweed patch and count the eggs, caterpillars, and adults you see each week for the Monarch Larva Monitoring Project. You'll help scientists learn where and why monarchs are doing well (and where they're in trouble).

If you live near a California overwintering site, you can join the Western Monarch Thanksgiving Count! Each year, thousands of people gather at roosting sites to help count monarchs so that scientists can track how many monarchs there are from year to year.

Support Organizations That Help Monarchs

Raise money for nonprofits like Monarch Joint Venture or their many partners. They use the funds to help people create pollinator habitat and study monarchs, and they teach people how to help monarchs.

How to Rear a Monarch

Watching a monarch grow and change is so much fun! If you are gentle, you can even hold a monarch without damaging its wings.

Rear just a few monarchs at once. Humans can't raise enough monarchs to help the population, and rearing too many in one place can spread diseases. Be sure to check for any rules or regulations about handling monarchs in your state.

1. Find a monarch caterpillar in the wild. Look carefully on milkweed leaves throughout the spring and summer. Never order monarchs from Internet suppliers. They can carry disease, and they may be genetically different from wild monarchs.

2. Find a clean container large enough for the monarch to emerge without hurting its wings. A large deli tub works great! Poke lots of small holes in the lid. If you rear more than one monarch, keep them in separate containers in case they are sick.

3. Collect fresh milkweed. For best results, pick the leaves, then rinse or soak them in water. Pat them dry and store them in the fridge between moist paper towels, in a plastic bag. These leaves will last for days. Wash your hands after handling milkweed so that you don't rub any of the milky latex in your eyes.

4. Put your caterpillar in the container with a moist (but not dripping) piece of paper towel or coffee filter in the bottom. Place a small twig, stick, or folded strip of screen in the container for the caterpillar to climb.

5. Give your monarch fresh milkweed every day. If it's a tiny larva, just place the old leaf it's on right on top of a fresh one. You can also use a paintbrush to nudge a small larva onto a new leaf.

6. Each day, remove your caterpillar, rinse and dry the container, and replace the moist paper towel with a fresh one until the monarch becomes a chrysalis.

Caterpillar poop is called frass, and monarchs make a lot of it! As adult butterflies, their waste is only liquid.

7. When your caterpillar is a big fat fifth instar, it will climb to the top of the container and get ready to "J." Keep your eyes peeled! Your monarch will become a chrysalis within a day. Watch it do the "pupa dance" as it wriggles out of its skin!

8. In 9 to 14 days, the chrysalis will turn dark. The butterfly is ready to emerge. Make sure there is nothing that will get in the way of its wings. If you get to see it eclose (emerge), look for the two parts of its proboscis that zip into one. It's the last thing to develop!

9. If your monarch falls as it emerges, simply offer a finger for its legs to grip and bring it to the top of the container. It will hold on to its pupa casing or silk pad while it pumps up its wings.

10. After 4 hours, you can let your monarch go. It's best to release your monarch on a sunny, warm day (60°F/16°C or warmer), near flowers. Or you can feed it some honey water on a clean cotton ball or sponge. For the honey water, mix 1 part honey with 4 parts water.

Note: Always sterilize your containers before using them again! A grown-up can help you rinse them with a solution of 10 percent chlorine bleach, or you can run them through the dishwasher on the "sanitize" cycle.

Hold a monarch's closed wings gently between your thumb and index finger.

Fun Facts

You might see monarchs and other butterflies drinking at shallow pools of water. This is called puddling. In Mexico, they sometimes puddle in large groups.

During World War II, Dr. Boris Berkman discovered that the seed fluff from milkweed pods was great for making life jackets float! Milkweed was an unsung hero for the United States during the war.

monarch

viceroy

Because they eat milkweed, monarchs don't taste good and can even be toxic to some predators who might eat them. The monarch's bright colors are like a message that says, *Don't eat me!* The viceroy butterfly has evolved to mimic, or look like, a monarch in order to fool predators. Can you see the difference between a monarch and a viceroy?

A butterfly pupa is called a chrysalis.

Most moths, on the other hand, make what is called a cocoon, a silk casing they spin around their bodies before they pupate.

Glossary

antennae. Sensory organs on a butterfly's head that help it smell

brood. A generation of monarchs

chrysalis. The pupa formed between the larval and adult stages of a butterfly or moth

claspers. Organs at the end of the adult male butterfly's abdomen used to hold the female during mating

cremaster. The hooklike tip of the pupa that holds it to a surface

eclose. To emerge into the adult stage as a butterfly

habitat. The natural home environment of a plant or animal, where its needs get met

hemolymph. Insect blood

instar. A period of growth a larva goes through between molts

larva. The immature stage of an insect; for butterflies and moths, this is the caterpillar stage

mandibles. The chewing mouthparts of the butterfly larva

maxillary palps. Organs on the head of the larva that help it smell and feel

metamorphosis. In an insect, the process of transformation from an immature form to an adult form

migrate. For animals, to travel from one habitat to another in order to survive the change of seasons

molt. When an animal sheds its skin, hair, fur, or shell

ocelli. The eyes of a larva

oviposit. When a female insect lays eggs

palpi. Ridges on the head of the adult monarch that help it smell

pesticide. A poison that is used to kill unwanted weeds and insects, often in farming and in managing mosquitoes

pollinate. To transfer pollen from one flower to another in the process of fertilization, allowing flowers to produce seeds

pollinator. An insect or other animal that, while feeding, carries pollen from one plant to another plant.

predator. An animal that eats another animal

proboscis. The long strawlike mouthpart of a butterfly, through which it drinks nectar and water

pupation. The stage during which a monarch is a chrysalis, developing from larva to adult

spinneret. The organ on a monarch larva's chin that allows it to spin silk thread

spiracles. Tiny holes in the sides of the larva, chrysalis, and butterfly that allow them to breath

tarsi. The feet of butterflies and other flying insects

tentacles. Filaments, or feelers, on the body of the larva that help it sense the world

CURRICULUM GUIDES FOR EDUCATORS

Monarch Joint Venture's *Monarchs and More* curriculum provides inquiry-based lessons and activities for both inside the classroom and outdoors. Separate guides for grades K–2, grades 3–6, and middle school include age-specific lessons divided into six sections on butterfly life cycles, butterfly systematics, ecology, conservation, conducting experiments, and monarch migration. Each guide also includes extensive background information and practical tips for rearing and observing insects. See https://monarchjointventure. org/mjvprograms/education/ monarch-education-resources.

Going Deeper

You can learn a lot more about monarchs! The following resources provide a wealth of information about many of the topics introduced in this book.

Milkweed

There are more than 100 species of milkweed in the United States. To learn more about milkweed and the many plants important to monarchs and other pollinators, see:

Xerces Society
https://xerces.org
- Monarch nectar plants by region and season
- Milkweed seed finder
- Identifying milkweed species native to your area

Monarch Health and Mortality

About 95 percent of a female monarch's eggs in the wild never make it to adulthood. This is very common in the insect world. There is no evidence that people rearing monarchs can increase monarch population numbers. But there is evidence that rearing large numbers of them may spread disease, modify migratory behavior, and affect genetics. The best way to help conserve monarchs is to build habitat for all stages of the monarch life cycle. For more information, see:

Monarch Joint Venture
https://monarchjointventure.org
- Gardening to support monarchs
- Rearing monarchs responsibly
- Monarch conservation best practices and longitudinal population data
- Monarch Larva Monitoring Project

Project Monarch Health
www.monarchparasites.org
- OE (*Ophryocystis elektroscirrha*) and other monarch parasitoids and diseases
- Participating in OE citizen science

Tagging Monarchs and Tracking Migration

Regular people have been helping to tag and observe monarchs for decades. Because of their good work, scientists were able to solve the mystery of where monarchs went in the wintertime. For more information about tagging and observing, and to learn how migration is tracked, see:

Journey North
https://journeynorth.org
- Tracking the migration of monarchs
- Contributing monarch observations
- Observing other animal migrations and seasonal changes

Monarch Watch
https://monarchwatch.org
- Tagging monarchs east of the Rocky Mountains
- Creating a Monarch Waystation

Southwest Monarch Study
www.swmonarchs.org
- Tagging monarchs in Arizona and the southwestern United States
- Migration data for monarchs in the southwestern United States
- Regional resources for gardening and finding milkweed

Monarch Alert
https://monarchalert.calpoly.edu
- Tagging monarchs in California
- Overwintering populations in California

Climate Change and Monarchs

Burning coal, oil, and gas for energy and transportation releases carbon dioxide and other gases that are changing the earth's climate. Farming practices and cutting down forests also contribute to climate change. Changes in the climate affect where and when milkweed and nectar plants grow, and the cues that tell monarchs when to migrate. They may affect the "just right" conditions at overwintering sites, too, causing oyamel fir trees to grow higher and higher up the mountains. Climate change also causes more severe weather, including storms, droughts, floods, and wildfires. For a kid-friendly resource on climate change, see:

NASA Climate Kids
https://climatekids.nasa.gov

Conservation in Mexico

Monarchs are very important to the people of Mexico. Much of their overwintering habitat is now part of the Monarch Butterfly Biosphere Reserve. Cutting trees in or near the reserve threatens monarchs. But the people who live nearby need firewood, lumber, and farm fields. One program that is helping both the forest and the people is the Monarch Butterfly Fund. This organization works to reduce illegal logging while encouraging forest recovery for the long-term health of these crucial overwintering sites. For more information, see:

Monarch Butterfly Fund
https://monarchconservation.org

Monarch Butterfly and Pollinators Conservation Fund
www.nfwf.org/programs/monarch-butterfly-and-pollinators-conservation-fund

Day of the Dead

Day of the Dead customs in Mexico are a blend of the ancient beliefs of the first peoples of the region and the rituals of the Catholic Spanish conquerors. The Aztecs and other native peoples saw death as a natural part of the cycle of life, and they had rituals and celebrations for honoring their ancestors. They saw butterflies as the living souls of the dead and also understood much about their life cycles. The Mazahua Indian name for the monarch butterfly means "daughter of the sun." The Spanish brought the ritual of adorning loved ones' graves with bread, favorite foods, and wine. For more about Día de los Muertos, see:

Day of the Dead Books for Kids
www.pbs.org/parents/thrive/day-of-the-dead-books-for-kids

Index

A

abdomen/abdominal segments, 8, 11, 14, 15
anatomy
    butterfly, 14–15
    caterpillar, 8–9
    chrysalis, 11
antennae, 9, 14, 15

B

bees, 18
bugs, 18–19
butterfly
    anatomy of a, 14–15
    male and female, 15, 20
    viceroy versus monarch, 42

C

California, migration and, 32, 39
caterpillar, 8–9
    finding, in the wild, 40
    larval life and, 6–7
    metamorphosis of, 10–11
    milkweed patch and, 19
    poop of (frass), 41
    rearing a monarch, 40–42
chrysalis, 43
    anatomy of a, 11
    darkening of, 12
    metamorphosis and, 10
cremaster, 11

D

danger, to monarchs, 34–35. See also
  predators
Day of the Dead (Día de los Muertos), 26–27

E

eggs, laying (oviposit), 5–6, 20, 31

F

facts, fun, 43
fall, 26–27
flight. See also migration, southern; migra-
    tion, western

final, 30–31
    first, 13
flowering trees and shrubs, 35
flowers, 21, 38. See also milkweed
    fall-blooming, 25
    western monarchs and, 32–33
fritillary, great spangled (butterfly), 18

H

habitat, 34, 36–37, 38. See also milkweed
hatching monarchs, 12–13
helping monarchs, 33, 38–39
hemolymph (insect blood), 13, 14
holding monarchs, 42

I

insects, 18–19. See also butterfly
instars, 6

L

larva/larval life, 6–7

M

mariposas (butterflies), 26–27
mating monarchs, 20, 30
metamorphosis, 10–11
Mexico
    migration and, 24, 26–27, 32
    ofrendas (altars) in, 26, 27
    puddling, water and, 43
    resting place in trees, 28–29
    springtime in, 30–31
migration, southern, 22–25
    distance per day, 23
    flowers with nectar for, 25
    Mexico destination, 24, 26–27
migration, western, 32–33
milkweed, 4–5, 16–17
    broods of monarchs and, 20
    chemicals and, 35
    habitat and, 38
    patches of, 18–19, 39
    tropical, monarch disease and, 38
molting, 6, 7

N

nectar, 21, 25

P

pesticides, 35
pollinators, 21, 35, 37
predators, 29, 34, 37
proboscis, 15, 21
puddling, water and, 43
pupa, butterfly. See chrysalis
pupation, 10

R

raising money for monarchs, 39
roosting, at night, 23

S

scales, 12, 14
scientist, citizen, 39
spinneret, 7, 9, 10
springtime, 30–31
summertime, 20–23

T

tagging monarchs, 39
tasting, with tarsi (feet), 14
thorax, 8, 14
trees, monarchs resting in, 23, 28–29

V

viceroy butterfly, 43

W

West, monarchs in the, 32–33
wings, 14, 15
    chrysalis and, 11
    hatching and, 12–13
    holding monarch's closed, 42
winter, monarchs in, 26, 28–29, 36–37, 39

The mission of Storey Publishing is to serve our customers by publishing practical information that encourages personal independence in harmony with the environment.

Edited by Alethea Morrison and Hannah Fries
Art direction and book design by Alethea Morrison
Text production by Kristy MacWilliams
Indexed by Christine R. Lindemer, Boston Road Communications
Illustrations by © Olga Baumert

Storey books are available at special discounts when purchased in bulk for premiums and sales promotions as well as for fund-raising or educational use. Special editions or book excerpts can also be created to specification. For details, please call 800-827-8673, or send an email to sales@storey.com.

Storey Publishing
210 MASS MoCA Way
North Adams, MA 01247
storey.com

Printed in China by R.R. Donnelley
10 9 8 7 6 5 4 3 2

Library of Congress Cataloging-in-Publication Data on file

For my beautiful boys. Henry and William, may you continue to find wonder in the natural world, notice the tiny things, and find the poems they write.

Acknowledgments

My deep gratitude to Karen Oberhauser for inviting me into the world of monarch butterflies so long ago, and for telling me to write this book. My gratitude to my talented editor, Hannah Fries, for her guidance and for making this book such a pleasure to write. Thank you to Katie-Lyn Bunney, Wendy Caldwell, Jerónimo Chávez, Carol Clark, Cathy Downs, Stephanie Turcotte Edenholm, Maria Eugenia González, Sarah Hobbie, Stephanie Lopez, Gail Morris, Cindy Peterson, Ellen Sharp, Marti Starr, and Kim Young for their expertise, friendship, and support. I am grateful to my husband, Jeff, for his steadfast encouragement. And thank you to my loving parents for making the natural world our playground.